EMINENCE

Poetry Book
Volume IV

Rian N. Jenkins

EMINENCE

Poetry Book
Volume IV

Rian N. Jenkins

Acknowledgments

I am forever grateful that God allowed me to flourish in a gift that is a generational blessing being shared with the world through publishing and spoken word performances!

To my mother who helped mold this queen into the woman I am today, I am appreciative of receiving the writing gene that was definitely inherited from you, and you have purchased every book released. When you can, you attend events, which include the panel discussions. I will never forget how I would find out at book fests (fairs) that you were talking me up to other authors and vendors.

To my Aunt Mary and Aunt Dell who have always been supportive of my craft and gift. You can count on my Aunt Mary and mother to be in the crowd for book fests (fairs) and panel discussions.

I am also thankful to other family members who have purchased books and/or attended performances.

I am thankful to my pastors, Bishop Herbert and Dr. Marcia Bailey, who always encourage us to maximize every gift God has placed in us to be light and salt to this world.

As I have grown in this gift, I am greatly appreciative to my author, poetry, and writing community which has grown over the past 30 years.

To Bugsy Calhoun and Wintah Storm who are also known as Jamal and Karen Washington and are some of my biggest cheerleaders: forever grateful for your encouragement, support, and constructive criticism.

To my Poetree Family: Tavern "TK Care" Hampton, Christopher "Chrisso" Blackmon, Brittany "ShaiMoonlight" Jones, Lorinda

"Morenike" Linen, Malika Daniels, Tiffany Brown, Shatoya White, Marie "Lyriq" Grady, and many more who have helped me grow as an artist and writer.

To Jennifer Bartell-Boykin, Columbia's Poet Laureate, and Tayler Simon, our literary superhero, I appreciate how I have grown and learned so much from both of you in regards to writing, advocacy, and social justice. You invite me into spaces or recommend me to people who provide opportunities that have propelled me professionally. I am forever grateful!

To both of my editors, Sharon Morgan and Marla Taviano: you pushed my creativity to another level. This book is better because of you.

Table of Contents

Consumed

Why am I consumed with you
So consumed with you
So consumed with you
So consumed I've lost my mind
My mind . . .
So consumed I've lost my mind

Obviously, I've lost my mind.
Grinning, bearing this heartache.
No one with common sense
        would accommodate foolishness
Invest this time, energy,
        into a heart reciprocating nothing.
Foolishly believing love is sacrificial.
Erasing myself from the equation.
Camouflaging into the woman you need.
Loneliness has convoluted my thinking.
Diluting my existence.
Disappearing won't allow me to feel any grievance.

Tolerating malnourishment.
Hunger has driven me to delusion,
        mistaking additives and preservatives as nutrition.
Satisfied with a piece,
        a slice of whatever remnant you're serving.
Craving whatever you're giving,
        what my soul has been missing.
Daddy was absent.
Momma was too caught up in chasing
        an image of him to listen,
        misinterpreting my love language.
The anguish in my soul to behold affection, attention.

Obviously, I'm consumed with you
So consumed with you
Desperation has created an unquenchable obsession,
    absurdly believing being with you is fulfilling.
This void continues to resemble an abyss,
    promises never coming to fruition.
Like clay, I am manipulated, disfigured
        to resemble a receptacle,
        making it acceptable to be devalued.
Becoming someone I said I would never be.
My mother's love life was never my dream.
Her nightmare morphed into my reality.
Replicating a generational curse.
Abdicating my throne.
Your majesty has chosen peasantry
        all because I want you to love me.

Why am I consumed with you
Truly consumed with you
Content with her residue on your lips.
How I abhor loneliness to the point
    I coddle the mismanagement of emotions.
My mother prays daily the cycle will end—
        "Please God help her to steer clear
        of any more captains
        who are pirates
        stealing from queens."
By any means, you profit from my weakness.
Sinking deep.
Who is going to save me?
The stench saturating my psyche
    doesn't have to be permanent.
Stagnant, I don't have to be.
Complacent, I don't have to be.

Never should I ignore my wants and needs.
Forgetting my worth surpasses the dollar value of
     diamonds
     rubies
     emeralds
     sapphires.
Never did I have to acquire my crown.
Born into royalty.
I don't have to settle for anything.
I don't have to settle for anything.
I don't have to settle for anything.

No longer consumed with you
No longer consumed with you
Can't afford to lose my mind, forsake my soul.
The power in me will allow me to reclaim my authority
     while abandoning the notion love requires
     the erasure of the essence
     of who God perfectly handwoven into His image.
Deserving abundance, not depletion.
Prosperity is what I should be welcoming.
Surrounded by Him.
Embraced forever in joy.
Never again will I be anyone's toy.
I am treasure.
Never hidden.
Good riddance to any joker
     who fooled himself into believing
     he reflected a king.
The King of Kings will teach me everything.
Agape, unconditional, unwavering love filling me up.
Whole and alert, discerning of potential heartbreak.
Whole and open to love,
     assessing and not assuming his capacity to love.

Breathing, living, moving as a warrior,
    a champion in purpose,
    a plan not involving man.
Never thirsty or hungry.
The table is always prepared with a feast.
Occupying my place.
Passionately shining my light.
Accepting and affirming the magnificence.
This tree with flowers blooming,
    branches dancing in the wind.
Strong, rooted into the source.
Boldly, intentionally living free.

Eminence

I am light.
Overpowering darkness.
Illuminating.
Radiating confidence.
This crown fits me perfectly.
Deemed worthy by the King.
He loves me.
Destined since the beginning of time.
Interwoven in my mother's womb.
Beautifully handcrafted for a purpose,
    my reason for dwelling on this earth.
He died for me,
    walked out of the tomb three days later,
    setting me free.
Equipping and strengthening this vessel
    to create and dominate.
I can't be overtaken, crushed, or destroyed.
Persevering through any pain, trial, tribulation.
Glorious victory outweighs the hurt.
Speaking life, resurrecting what was deemed dead.
Bestowing keys to anyone who seeks freedom.
Reigning in every arena assigned to my journey.
A fortress only trusting in Him who created me.
His Masterpiece.

Unconventional
(extended Haiku)

Never meant to fit.
Too legit to settle for
normal; only dope.

The road less traveled
while hearing I am so wrong
to end in triumph.

Using the lessons
of my ancestors to build
invent, create new.

Undeniable
My Mother's (Barbara Jenkins) Educational Journey

Determined since the first grade
    to one day impact the multitude
    through a classroom.
Witnessing the magic of cultivating genius.
Insistent no child will be humiliated, neglected.

Determined since the first grade
    to honor my parents.
Excellence with grades,
    good manners was the expectation.
The preparation was needed to punch my ticket.
Eighth grade class valedictorian.
Number six out of all the high school graduates
    granted me full access.

Determined since the first grade
    to never be forced in a seat
    to fill a quota.
Some made history, opened the doors for many.
I couldn't sacrifice an educational experience
    only meant to be enjoyable and enriching.
I had to thrive where I was
    wanted
    appreciated
    valued.
Two opportunities were dismissed to
    "better" my education,
    be one of the firsts to progress this nation.

Trusted my process
    my instinct

my intellect.
I will flourish wherever I am planted.
My mother was infuriated but later accepted
        I was determined.

One of the oldest historical Black universities and colleges
        imparted knowledge,
        molding and equipping this young woman
        who will forever be celebrated for being
        an orchestrator of greatness.
A lighthouse guiding many ships into the shores of education.
Many will attribute their growth, success
        to this once first grader who was determined
        to exhibit her magnificence and prominence.

Ode to Capresha

Yes, in the midst of grief,
we must remind ourselves
death's sting is nonexistent.
Our sister never gave up the fight.
Victorious, she is!

We can celebrate the evidence of His goodness.
He won!
She won!
Hearing *well done, my good and faithful servant.*
Dancing in heaven and rejoicing.
Marveling at our Majesty in all His glory.
Crying holy, holy, holy
to our Lord God Almighty.

The Lord who gave us a vessel.
Purposed with a plan to illuminate this Earth.
Darkness was eradicated with her presence.
A sweet fragrance lingering in the atmosphere.
An aroma that possesses an undeniable power.

A true reflection of our Father's magnificence
Eminence
Brilliance
Excellence.

Wholeness
        is the cadence
        this godly woman struts in.
Living unapologetically.
Radically, powerfully, and
        fully unashamedly a disciple of Christ.

A daughter of Zion,
       unconditionally poured into God's people.
Infusing our spirits, our souls.
Encouraging us
       to chase,
       to seek
the Father who will continually,
       unconditionally love us.

Girls transformed into women,
       whole women because of her wisdom.
Awakening us, reminding us of our authority.

Men and women were
       strengthened ...
       uplifted ...
       empowered ...
       inspired ...
       by the fire blazing from her soul.
Never could it be controlled.
An inferno blazing a trail,
       followed by many,
       a legacy carried on by those who will echo
       love and compassion, drawing more to Him.

For Trayvon
Born Day Celebration (February 5th)

On this day,
    a prince was born,
    soon to be king
    who should have grown
    to witness his full potential.
His greatness overtook this world.
His dream should not have been deferred.
Snuffed out by hatred.
He should be celebrating his birth on earth.
Another descendant of royalty
    who was regarded as peasantry.

His parents are adamant he will live on.
Refusing to rest in bitterness.
Countless parents are living the same nightmare.
Legislation acts as if they are unaware.
Unable to consistently prohibit
    the disregard of Black lives.
We can never grow weary.
Must tell the story.
Fighting until glory presents itself
    from this affliction against humanity.

Princes deserve to live on to be kings.
Princes deserve to live on to be kings.
Princes deserve to live on to be kings.

We won't let them forget him.

We will continue to fight until all Black lives matter.

I BE BLACK

I am BLACK.
I be that BLACK chick,
    that BLACK woman,
    that BLACK queen.
I am BLACK.
Let's spell that
    B-LACK.
I be that one who don't lack nothing.
I be that one who don't lack intelligence.
I be that one who don't lack eminence.
I be that one whose presence is wrapped in glory.
I represent the story of my ancestors
    who want us to reclaim
    our places on the throne.
I represent the lineage of kings and queens
    who exude power.
Never will I devour anyone's vilification
    of my humanity.

Unapologetically declaring
    I am
    I be
    I will always be BLACK.
Not being dismissive of the label African American.
It is just something about boldly saying,
    I AM BLACK.
Owning the color that some deem dark,
    not referring to the richness of my melanin
    but dark in the sense of representing
    an evil or vile presence as in
    denying the goddess.
    God created all of us in His image.

My purpose is to shine a light,
        boldly and bright.
        I am BLACK.

I ain't slacking.
I am that good thing
        they wish
        they hope
        they need.
I be not lacking beauty.
Copycats plump lips, hips
        mimicking figures
        once mocked,
        heckled into caricatures.
Seeking authenticity
        yet duplicating horribly
        what they will never be:
        BLACK.

BLACK ain't lacking magic.
I am full of it.
I am overflow.
I am excellence you wish to know.
I be not lacking ability.
I am ingenuity.
Orchestrator of excellence.
I am influence.
I am trend.
I am legacy.
I am longevity.
I be not lacking strength.
I withstand every hardship, injustice
        to rise higher than a phoenix.

My ashes morph into a cape
  flapping in the wind,
  destroying all stereotypes,
  nullifying every lie
  I need to colonize to make it.
Again, I am BLACK.
Let's spell that.
I BE LACK, I lack nothing.

We Believe in You

Black boy . . .
Black man . . .
        I need you to understand
        you are a king.
I don't care how
        they demean your being,
        belittle what God has deemed magnificent.
They keep labeling you as a threat.
Subservient to their ill-conceived
        stereotypes and prejudices.
Dismissive of the fact they stole you, us
        from a land where we ruled and thrived.
The existence of your life
        threatens their cowardly dominance.

The same God who created them created us.
Adam was the first.
Out of dust, God breathed His perfection,
        created in the image
        only associated with eminence.
Your melanin is a powerful symbol of greatness!
Yes, royalty is your namesake!
None of
        the vile names
        laws
        policies
        systems
        they create
        nullifies you are a conqueror, warrior.
Never question your ability.
Empowered to handle anything.

The crown has always been yours.
Heavy at times.
Your queens are here to hold you.
Reminding you that
    the brilliance of your mind,
    the perseverance of your spirit
    goes back thousands of generations.
When they had Jim Crow laws,
    you built flourishing businesses, cities, towns.
Despite being bombed and burned down,
    we arose from the ashes.
Marched on,
continued growing our lineage,
our legacy.

There is a long list of prominent roles you have inhabited:
    inventors
    engineers
    teachers
    bankers
    lawyers
    artists
    doctors
    dentists
    Senators
    Congressmen
    and the President.

Prosperity is the language we continue to speak
    despite our grief and anguish.
Still fighting the same war
    to just live freely in equity.
Our potential has always been exponential.
The sky isn't the limit when

the moon is something you play with.
My king, we need you to keep going.
We are behind you and with you.
We support and love you.
We believe in you.

Don't Call It Unfair

Saying that racism is unfair
　　doesn't quite measure the level of disgust.
What did we do to deserve this?
We can't just say it is unfair.
Unfair is
　　you putting down a DRAW TWO
　　when you know I just said UNO.
Unfair is
　　when you clearly didn't touch the base,
　　and the umpire screams you are safe.
Unfair is
　　I must share my toy
　　with my younger sister who just drools on it.
　　Annoyed!
　　No appreciation.

What I can't call unfair is
　　how the prayers covering our children
　　beg for the blood to cover them,
　　so they are not mistaken as the next suspect,
　　fitting the profile to meet a quota.

We can't call it unfair
　　when there is apprehension,
　　when the blue lights are flashing,
　　when we pass by three, four cops pulling over one car.
I shouldn't be momentarily paralyzed in fear,
　　pleading with God to make it home.

Devaluing humans isn't being unfair.
Try unfathomable.
Incomprehensible.

Disturbing.
Unraveling.
Yet, we still manage to thrive,
    pushing and pressing despite our souls grieving.
Bewilderment,
    our lives have yet to matter.
The tap water in our communities shouldn't be poisoned.
Our infrastructure in the United States of America,
    the land of opportunity,
    shouldn't mirror developing countries.
This land that will hand out billions to Ukraine,
    others across this world who are fighting wars,
    yet there are wars outside our doors,
    grocery shopping or attending school,
    haunted by guns more available than vegetables.
Unfortunately, eradicating violence isn't the mission
    when the guns and drugs fund white collar thugs.
Neglecting schools lacking quality facilities and teachers
    to overcrowd prisons to maintain slave culture.
The betterment of our society has been diminished
    to overstuffing bank accounts rather than
    growing exponentially in intellect.
Crazily, the orchestrator of hatred
    has the nerve to cry out in despair that
    we are undeserving of higher-level positions,
    equal representation in major stores like Walmart and Target,
    equal footing when it comes to admissions.

Unjustified.
Evil acts against humanity aren't just aggravating.
Agonizing our spirit.
More than equipped to sustain the ill treatment.
Nevertheless, brilliant beings shouldn't be subjected
    to our tolerance level being tested.

Magnificent not just due to our intellect.
We don't lower ourselves to your level of vileness.
We refuse to quit.
We have always been legit.
Never will we succumb to your plan
        to control, stifle, or annihilate our existence.
Refuse to forfeit any demand to live the life
        our ancestors so beautifully flourished.
You can't force kings and queens to enjoy peasantry.
We will rise.
And you will see it's more than unfair:
        Unfathomable—
        the people you want to eradicate
        didn't turn our hate
        that we could easily give you
        the fate you rightfully deserve.

Shatterproof

I won't bow.
I won't break.
I won't stumble.
I won't fall.
Boldy standing tall.
Declaring my eyes are fixed.
Determined to keep winning
        despite the opposition
        that finds a new way to attempt to dethrone me.
My lineage runs thick through my veins.
Longer than the Nile.
My ancestors have traveled so many miles,
        built too many bridges for me to cross
        for me to scorch them,
        leaving another generation lost.
Created with a purpose.
Destined for greatness,
        making it impossible to
        bow
        break
        stumble
        fall.
Boldly standing tall.
Our eyes are fixed.
Winning with every step.

Rainbows Without Sunshine

Someone asked me today,
 Why you ain't smiling?
 Babygirl, I know you got a beautiful smile.
 Show off that beauty, lady.
As if this frown on my face dims my light,
 erasing the fact I illuminate this earth.

Why can't I display my true emotions?
Don't feel like dressing up for the masquerade today.
Momentarily, I am allowed to be in my feelings.
Sometimes I know this light affliction
 won't compare to the glory,
 but today my story is
 I refuse to be phony,
 shuck and jive when I am not alright.

Maybe everything is okay
 but my face just reverberates focus.
On a mission to accomplish everything God promised.
Fulfilling the assignment doesn't require a smile.
The joy of my soul strengthens me to keep going.

Either way, I should be able to grace
 this earth without a smile from time to time
 without you sadly attempting to drop lines.
Why do women always have to come off as
 approachable
 palatable
 tolerable
 manageable.

Never can make anyone feel uncomfortable.
No longer seeking to appease you.
Digestible I can't be.
Strength makes you queasy.
Just let a sister be.

Resolute

My tears won't fall.
They hold on.
Harnessing strength witnessed
    from my ancestors
    sitting at counters enduring heckling
    and assaults in the form of
    dumping of condiments and hurling of fists.
Can't cry anymore.
We've been here too many times before.
Our stance will never waver
    until we savor the glory
    you obstruct with your afflictions—
    the blatant disregard for humanity.
Honoring our royal heritage is the resilience
    fueling the fight that demands equitable change.
Refusing to succumb to your venomous hatred,
    contorting your mouth to spew beliefs
    despite how asinine it seems:
    we should go back where we came from.
Never asked to be here.
Forced into enslavement.
You destroyed dynasties.
Beaten or killed by those who uphold the law,
    rules and regulations only inflicted
    to continue to imprison us
    who just wanted equity.
Never expected special privileges.
Protecting our existence.
Both of our hearts beat while bleeding red.
Yet, you declare the hue in your complexion
    makes you superior to our melanin.
We are not your enemy.

We are not a threat.
We are not servants.
We built this country.
We won't die without our inheritance:
      life and the pursuit of happiness.
Despite your excessive, unconscionable,
      vile ignorance,
      moronic rhetoric,
      we will not stop declaring:
      hate won't win.
Unstoppable
Undeniable
Unapologetically exuding our fire.

Halo of Glory

Naturally
Unapologetically
I rock a halo of glory.
Crowned
Beauty
Nappy
Kinky
Curly.

Fearfully, wonderfully made.
Never to cast shade
on my sisters who rock
their hair in other ways.
Healthy hair is the goal.
Our melanin is gold.
Shining bright.
Diamonds can't come close.
They lack our luster and value.

Naturally
Unapologetically
Rock a halo of glory.
Crowned
Beauty
Nappy
Kinky
Curly
Fearfully, wonderfully made.

Legacy

Black people are so cool.
Black people are so dope.
Don't you dare
      associate or define our existence
      with anything less than eminence.
Brilliance.
Black people are resilient.
Building and creating while you
      hating and creating legislation
      only meant to castrate.
We never needed your handout
      after you destroyed our kingdoms.
Our mindsets never shifted.
We always showed up, bossed up.
Some are still waiting for their turn.
I need them to learn
      a lot of people didn't wait to be called up.
They just stood up,
      shouted, shined,
      reigned supreme.
Exhibiting the essence of our being as geniuses.
Masterpieces with a value no buyer can outbid.
Giants, kings, queens who will
      outlive, override
      any attempt to deny our rights.
Generations are standing, thriving, exhibiting
      what our ancestors believed and achieved.

Unveiling

Poem written for James Baldwin's 100th Birthday Celebration

Why do we carry the young into spaces
    to witness brilliance
    they may not remember,
    may not cherish or relish,
    embrace like a desired toy?

Maybe we will awaken a space
    in their heart that is dormant.
Unknowing or cognizant of the potential
    of what can grow if we expose
    young eyes and minds to a future
    they didn't know existed.

Culture is what it is giving.
Experiences that are life-changing.
Igniting a passion, a dream to be lived as reality.
Inspiring, empowering, impacting.
Reverberating in the souls and spirits of many,
    a contagious energy elevating,
    illuminating this earth.

Maybe we also understand
    we can never be content with saying
    he or she is the first
    with no one standing in line
    to pass the baton, the legacy.
We beam with pride as they roll their eyes.
We carry them into spaces
    to witness magnificence.
Permeating their psyche with images
    alternating destiny.

Igniting a passion, a dream to be lived as reality.
Inspiring, empowering, impacting.
Reverberating in the souls and spirits of many,
    a contagious energy elevating,
    illuminating this earth.

Maybe we sense the gift God placed in their spirit.
Cultivation and irrigation are needed for it to sprout.
We ignore the pouts on their faces
    when we carry them into spaces
    to witness eminence,
    identifying the journey God has for them.
Igniting a passion,
    a dream to be lived as reality.
Inspiring, empowering, impacting.
Reverberating in the souls and spirits of many,
    a contagious energy elevating,
    illuminating this earth.

We Said No: The Mantra of Supreme Beings

We said no.
No, I don't want your goods to kidnap my brothers and sisters.
No, I would rather drown than be captive.
No, I would rather kill the captain to loosen my shackles.
No, I would rather risk losing my limbs learning to read, running to
     freedom.
No, I will not leave my brothers, my kings, and sisters, my queens, to die
as enslaved beings.
No, you can't claim that you are the architects of this country.
No, I won't stay silent, so I will run for office.
No, I won't farm your land for nearly pennies.
No, I will not live in a town where I own nothing.
No, I won't sit in the back of the bus.
No, I won't be compliant and accept that my vote doesn't matter.
No, I won't allow you to defile us by telling us where we can't go to
     school.
No, we will no longer be restricted to ghettos and slums when you have
     the nerve to have us sing the tune "this land is my land."
No, I won't stand with my head held high beaming in my achievement
     while my people lack power, equity, and continue to be lynched.
No, we won't keep walking in the back door to be adored by fans who
     know I had to get dressed in a closet.
No, I can't accept that we are not mainstream artists.
No, I am not willing to sell albums without my face on the cover.
No, I can no longer sing for segregated audiences.
No, we will not accept division; the vision is to come together with all
     our resources.
No, I will not straighten my hair for television.
No, you can't take the credit for our inventions.
No, I will not fight in a war representing genocide while fighting for a
     country that doesn't recognize the value of my life.

No, I will not stop fighting for the right to vote, then help my people
create and sustain wealth.

No, I will not stop until I am the first Black woman in Congress and the
first Black person to run for President.

No, I will not accept you defiling my style to mimic it for profit.

No, I will not accept that an important, yet fictitious, character, Uhura,
will be the only Black woman astronaut.

No, I will not play any position other than quarterback.

No, I will not stop kneeling until our mothers stop screaming due to
senseless violence like police brutality.

No, I will not stop believing in my dream because you called us
colorful cockroaches.

No, I will not let your lack of invitation to the CMAs stop me from
rocking my own stage.

No, I will not attend your inauguration, nor give explanation.

No, I won't give you a tour of the Vice President's residence.

No, I will not smile in the face of a President who hates my people.

No, I won't change the story proving we are worthy of budgets, stages,
and screens that yield billions.

No, I can't stop being who I am created to be:
A SUPREME BEING.

Royalty

I stand in the presence of royalty.
Future kings and queens,
    don't let anyone
    demean your being,
    belittle what God deemed magnificent.

Our melanin beams perfectly
    from any hue or complexion.
No shade is more superior.
Purposely and meticulously
    created by God.
There is no mistaking
    our existence is significant.
Our crown fits us perfectly.
Designed to fit despite the errors in judgment.
Never should we hold our head down.
Never desire to be anyone else.
No one can mirror our shine.
No one can copy our glow.

We are the essence of what
    causes this world to spin.
As it is necessary to breathe,
    we need to believe deep down within,
    exemplify the truth of our greatness.
When people try to tell us what we can't do,
    we remember we are gods, goddesses. God made us in His image.
Little gods on the earth.
Enabling us with the ability to do anything.
Yes, it is He Who strengthens you and me.
Our birth came with a plan to prosper.
A purpose: building wealth.
Cultivate that talent, that passion.

Our eminence goes back thousands of generations.
Nations that built cities.
Nations created inventions,
    sometimes amid deadly opposition.
There is no excuse for you
    not to display your gifts.
Talented
Brilliant
Inventive.
Yes, we are a threat.
Confusing the naysayers
    who don't believe in our power.
Dismantling their ill-conceived myths with our resilience.
Don't succumb to their ignorance.
Excellence and success are attainable.
Sometimes hard but attainable.
We must believe.
Put in the work.
Remember rewards outweigh pain.
Only associate your name and likeness
    with supreme beings.

Again, I bow in your presence.
I stand in awe of my young kings and queens.

Walk Away

Sometimes you must turn and walk away.
Purposely walk in another direction.
Intentionally
not facing
no longer embracing
ignoring
the liars, haters, backstabbers
seeking to belittle
or shatter the dreams
filled with promise and purpose.
Fearless with no regrets.
God empowered you.
God strengthened you.
God created you for this.
Keep strutting, Sis.
Know it is not worth the drama.
Stick to your path.
You will have the last laugh
when they end up sitting at the table
He prepared for you.

Peace

Some people underestimate the power of peace.
Peace isn't *I don't know.*
Peace is *I know.*
It is well with my soul.
There are certain things out of my control.
Who am I to get into a fray all
        because I am afraid of something
        that is nothing
        to the One who is omnipotent?

Peace is sometimes being quiet.
I don't have to respond,
        allow my emotions
        to get entangled in your turmoil.
Poisoning my spirit.
Blinding me to the promises
        resounding yes and amen.
I can be still.
No response needed.
No clapback is necessary.
My silence is golden.
My silence is enough retribution for any confusion.

Peace is *I don't understand it.*
His plan is bigger than what my mind can comprehend.
Depending on Him to steer me through the question marks.
I don't have to know all the answers.
I don't have to know where this path will lead.
As my guide, there are no mishaps or missteps.

Peace is *I am not anxious.*
He is the Author and Finisher of my faith.

He is Alpha and Omega, the Beginning and the End.
He is omniscient, knows all things.
Who am I to worry?

Peace equates to trust.
Trust in the Creator.
The one who wrote out my pages,
    the most beautiful story.
Mapped out my journey,
    my most glorious voyage,
    a prosperous plan for me.

Doesn't mean I won't face strife.
Doesn't mean I won't sacrifice.
I know in the end there is a great reward.
I chose life, not death.
I chose my God and not my flesh.
I chose peace.

Forward

I can't sit and wonder
if I made the right decision.
I can't sit and wonder
whether I missed it.
I can't look back anymore.
I can't sit and regret.
Flash back to a better ending.
Realizing there's a future
with a better outcome.
Hope is always present.
A promise with small beginnings
leading to great increase.
My God never changed
His plans for me.
Plans to prosper
if I just look forward.

Determined

Published in *Jasper Project* (online magazine) — Sundays with Jasper
Poetry of the People with Al Black

Determined.
He was fleeing.
With raindrops streaming down his face
        attempting to be an obstacle
        deterring him from the finish line.
Crying too many times almost eroded the lifeline.
Almost isn't none.
A little is much.
A mustard seed is enough to keep going.
Despite the sun not shining,
        he finally saw the light,
        his way out.
His breakthrough is attainable, worth the fight.

Determined.
Marching down the busiest road.
Bumper to bumper traffic doesn't stop him
        from rolling two suitcases, one with a broken wheel,
        along with the weight of two more bags,
        one on his back wasn't enough to defer his dream,
        obtaining the reality of freedom.
Pausing only to catch his breath.
He would not abort the mission.

Determined.
Nothing was going to stop him.
The raindrops are falling,
        creating what some would deem
        a collision course with reckless drivers.

Rainy days evoke a clash of wills,
    provoking fatigue among the weak.
Intimidated out of the belief of worthiness.
Determined, deserving of every promise.
He refused to get tired.
He knows he is strong enough to withstand rain.
The pain of staying is enough to push anyone insane.

Determined.
He wouldn't remain, waste away, abandon hope.
This rain didn't compare to the storm he faced for years.
He didn't care how many breaks he had to take.
He didn't care about onlookers wondering where he was going.
Ignoring their annoyance echoing in the blaring of horns.
He knows his destination.
Endless cycles of stagnation were no longer an option.

Determined.
Resilience is the cape flying behind him,
    undergirding him
    to pull two suitcases, one with a broken wheel,
    the weight of two more bags, one on his back
    wasn't enough to defer his dream,
    obtaining the reality of freedom
    through a busy street
    some would deem a borderline highway
    scaring away any boldness.
Yet, he is careful to avoid traffic.
Nothing was going to stop him from this journey.
Determined.

ACCOMPLISHED
Longleaf Middle School Eighth Grade Promotion 2023

Proud is the sentiment permeating this atmosphere.
You are here.
You finished.
Destined to win from the beginning.
An accomplishment speaking the truth:
    nothing can stop you.
Greatness flows through you.
Significant despite the circumstances.
Your brilliance reigns supreme.
In the heat of the pandemic,
    you thrived or barely survived.
Nevertheless, we celebrate
    you are on the other side.
    STANDING
    PROVING
    you are resilient.
Again, let this moment be a testament
    you always possessed
    what it takes to prevail.
Your crown fit you perfectly from birth.
Your emergence on this Earth spoke of eminence.
There is no ending to the success you will experience.
There are more accomplishments to revel in.
Achievements attained either through
    sweatless effort or with sweat and tears.
Never fear the process.
Always remember
    why you started.
Victory will outshine the hard times.
Wins in the midst of losing,
    learning while revealing

you are
BRILLIANTLY
BEAUTIFULLY
BOLDLY
OVERCOMING every opposition.
Proving again you are
STRONG
POWERFUL
UNSTOPPABLE
VALUABLE.

My Source

College-educated
but I am not dependent on the paper
people try to convince you
is the only way to add zeroes to your account.
My source is the Lord—
Provider,
Savior,
Giver of life,
Protector from strife,
Deliverer,
Father,
my everything
Who gave me the ability to earn that degree.
I can achieve anything in Him.
Unrestricted.
Uninhibited.
Limitless.
A degree isn't the only depiction of greatness.

This Man Said He Loves Me

This man said he loves me.
I'm not talking about that artificial, superficial love me.
    Sporting me as his trophy, not a partner or friend.
I'm not talking about
    that conditional where if I mess up he leaves.
I'm talking about that unconditional,
    never going away
    despite us going astray constantly.
The ultimate ride-then-die,
    sacrificing for all the sake of humanity
    even though He wanted the cup to pass.
Taking on a burden that was never His to carry.
I'm talking about the One Who did not sit behind the tomb.
The One who rose again, making me a joint heir with Him.
I am His friend.
Our connection makes me brand new.
That kind of love.

The mess-ups do not undo His affection toward me.
His thoughts toward me outnumber the grains of sand
    bordering the oceans and seas.
He only sees what-God-created-me-to-be-type love.

Never did I have to earn or beg for mercy,
    despite burning bridges He would rebuild.
Unfathomable, incomprehensible type of love.
That never-ending, run-on-sentence-with-multiple-misspellings-that-
    grammatically-don't-make-sense-yet-excels-type love.

I'm talking with that kind of love
    when the doctor says there's nothing else he can do,
    He says no boo I'm not through with you.

Through His love, we marvel at the miracle resurrecting,
     causing people to be amazed at His love.
Overjoyed and flabbergasted at loved ones
     who walked away from car wrecks unscathed.
Addictions that once wreaked havoc
     being broken in an instant due to His love.
I'm talking about
     that type of love that causes even the heart to mend
     in the midst of the craziest outbreak of heartache.
Galvanizing me to say there is a God who loves me.

The type of love that doesn't cause me to curse,
     not speaking ill of my neighbor.
I realize my tongue can speak either
     curses and death or life and favor.
Seeking to only lift all.
Breaking any bondages.
Speaking those things into existence.
I'm talking about
     that kind of love I can declare
     into the atmosphere—
     what I want according to His will.
He will see it so.
I'm talking about that
     kind of love that will not withhold any good thing from me.
Yes, that kind of love.

I'm talking about
     that kind of love that would not let me sit in poverty.
Yes, that man loves me to the point
     that he makes sure I have no needs.
He is the Lord God, my Shepherd.
I shall not want.

If I put in the work,
　　I will find myself in prosperity,
　　enriching all around me, bringing those up with me.
Yes, I'm talking about that kind of love.

That kind of love that causes me to flaunt, brag on His goodness.
Yes, I'm talking about that kind of love that is meant for all.
Never have to fight for his admiration.
I always have his undivided attention,
　　along with angels standing at attention waiting, ready.
Yes, that Man loves me.

I can never go too low or too high to escape this Man's love.
His never-wavers-for-anyone-type love.
That forever-His kind of love.
Sticking closer than a brother.
Loving harder than a father or mother.
Never forsaking me.
Always strengthening me.
Yes, this Man loves me.

Great

I don't expect you to get me.
Trendsetter I am.
I only follow the Master's plan.
Opposite of the norm.
The world I will change.
Never about knowing my name.
Just being what my Father called me to be:
GREAT.

Influencer
(extended haiku)

It is more than a
wave, trend, fad, easily gone.
Impact that lasts years.

Enlarging domains
People can't remain the same
when graced by brilliance.

Awakening those
seeking to inhabit their
magnificence too.

Be Your Sister's Keeper

Women who you deem silly
        don't need your pity.
Women who you deem worthless
        don't need your gossip.
They need to be
        uplifted
        empowered
        poured into.
Reminded of that same God
        Who created us in His likeness,
        making our worth infinite.
Reminded of their eminence.
Reminded of the power they possess.

Our pity, our gossip is dethroning, debilitating,
        enabling the devil to keep his foot on their neck.
We need to break his grasp.
As you see them sinking,
        I need you not to see them
        as incapable of the same grace you are granted daily.
Rather than viewing them as beneath you,
        see them as seeds
        desperately needing us to remove
        anything stunting growth.
Cultivating and tilling the soil.
Irrigating them with wisdom,
        repotting them in bigger spaces,
        allowing growth while embracing,
        being assured they are worth
        every good and perfect thing
        our Father promised.

Righteous actions aren't needed
        to complete the transaction of salvation.
Just be.
Exist.
Believe in His gift.
Eventually adapting to the habits,
        actions endowed in authority.
Recognizing they are royalty.
Operating in their purpose.
Honoring their significance.
Walking boldly while exuding His love.
Revealing they were never silly.
Just in need of sisters to be their keeper.

QUEENDOM (extended)

Despite the
    mistakes
    circumstances
    abuse
    mistreatment
I am a queen.
Born a princess.
Given dominion to reign.
Grace this world with my
    elegance
    brilliance
    beauty.
Uplifting those around me.

I refuse to embrace the term
    others want to call themselves: *a bad* ______
(You fill in the blank.)
Can't comprehend using any derogatory word
    the world wants to use as empowerment.
I refuse to put any of those words in my sentences.
I can't associate with any negative definition
    when my God wonderfully, beautifully
    created me in His image.
Again, from the beginning of time,
    He deemed this once girl a princess,
    now a queen.
Why would I demean anything
    only associated with greatness?
I cannot renounce my crown.

Sometimes people use those labels,
    mimicking their surroundings.

Examples who are either
    exhibiting generational blessings or curses.
Generational blessings and curses are taught
    consciously and unconsciously.

Generational blessings will have them
    looking toward the sky with their head held high.
Radiating an infectious energy.

Generational curses will have them
    hanging their head low,
    questioning every move,
    not believing they are worthy of anything.
Conveying a misconception of queendom:
    not being a woman of substance,
    only caught up in selfish ambition.

Either they love themselves,
    wholeness is their portion,
    or they need validation,
    always needing to be filled.
Either occupying the title
    go-getter
    trendsetter
    trailblazer
    inventor
Or settling for the scraps and handouts,
    subservient to someone else's purpose.
Embodying a level of class in my attire,
    setting fire to any stereotypes.
Partnering with a king versus a joker.

Queens, we must acknowledge our illumination
    is nourishment for our princesses.

The earth's harvest is predicated on our actions.
No longer can we declare for them
>to do as we say and not as we do
>when they see what we do,
>emulating our actions
>whether or not they want to.
Being a role model is not optional.

When they are out-of-pocket,
>don't be afraid to love them,
>uproot that seed seeking to corrupt them.
Again, speak life into them.
Love covers a multitude of sins.
Princesses can't win if they don't receive wisdom.
Don't be afraid to correct them.
They need us!

If by chance you were never taught,
>never gained that true definition of queendom
>from our Father in Heaven.
Seek Him and all His righteousness.
He will bestow an accurate definition,
>helping other princesses
>clearly see what it means to be a queen.
By any means, we can't allow this world to spin
>without being powered by our brilliance.
Elegance and wisdom must be passed down to multiple generations.

You Are a Queen, Too

I will not subject myself to your
        negative opinions,
        misguided judgment.
Maybe we should call it what it really is:
        perverted admiration.
Maybe you want to be me.
Lady, Queen,
        there's no need
        when you were also created in
        God's brilliant, beautiful image,
        cloaked in greatness.

Queen, no one can do you better than you.
There is no reason for you to hate on me
        or what I should be
        and wonder why you can't be.
You were never meant to mirror my puzzle piece.
We were never meant to be molded,
        taking on the likeness of a place
        we were only temporarily meant to inhabit
        while subduing.
Never destined to be imprisoned,
        paralyzed by competition.
Mirroring a system we didn't design.
A system capitalizing on our demise,
        reflecting a dysfunctional sisterhood.

Our light should be shining so brightly,
        darkness flees at our shadow.
Being fake doesn't reflect our love language.
Our tongues are not daggers
        or shovels burying our sisters.

Our words should uplift.
Our purpose, our existence should only construct
        peace
        endearment
        roses
        rainbows.
Impacting generations to follow.
Building legacies.
Never questioning a queen's happiness, wholeness.

No need to be heartless.
Don't allow the hate in your heart—
        the inability to see the greatness in you.
Wounded,
        scars have blinded you to your beauty.
Queen, you are beautiful.
Unleash the light screaming to radiate your eminence.
Your shine is needed.

You have a power,
        a responsibility to display preeminence.
Everything your hand touches shall prosper.
Made in the image of your Father.
Author and Finisher Who destined
        you
        we
        all to win.
There is no need for competition.
We can all sit at the table and eat.

You are
        strong
        brilliant
        influential

regal.
Let's embrace each other's crown.
Reigning as one.

Queens, Unite

When Queens unite,
the earth reaps its beauty.
Sisterhood illuminating
the lives of others.
Our princesses need us.
United,
standing strong as a fortress,
blocking the dark forces
from tainting what God
calls beautiful.

Courage

Courage is . . .
fear shouting in your ear,
seeking to intimidate.
Yet, you refuse to relinquish
your belief in the promise.
Persisting,
not drowning in the circumstances.
Surfing the waves of certainty,
your God equipped you to finish.

Educator
(extended haiku)

The undervalued
yet pivotal and vital
for the world to be.

The orchestrator,
cultivator of all the
brilliance and greatness.

No amount will be
enough to reward hearts of
gold BUT pay up now.

Don't Give Up

Sometimes I wonder how long the sirens must blare
        for you to be aware,
        notice something is wrong.
How many smoke screens ...
How many flares must blast ...
        for you to notice
        something, someone is in dire emergency?

A lot of times there are so many signs,
        so many cries for help.
Sometimes people are too involved in themselves
        to notice any wounded among them
        when they are distressed.
Sometimes trust is absent when family is negligent.
Don't expect them to help me.

Petitioning those who have the capacity to see ...
        I don't open up too easily.
Patience and grace is needed
Fighting demons that feast on my soul.
Yet, I need you to remain hopeful.
Don't give up on me.
Keep fighting.
Resuscitating the power within me.
Buried underneath the pain and anguish,
        I can't see the sunlight.
I can't feel the warmth of its rays.
The chirping of birds is drowned out by
        my thoughts rattling back and forth in my head,
        replaying all negative thoughts that were said.

Invoke the king or queen I can't see.
Awaken me to my purpose.
Enlighten me to redemption and recompense.
Engulfed in darkness blinds me to any light.
Too many times, I have been patched together
        with no expectation of recovery.

Believe in me.
Keep pushing.
Pray and advocate.
See me.
Help.
Help me to see myself.

His People Are Our People

Why are you so quick to call me out of my name?
Why are you so quick to call people out of their names?
Bury us with words, then wonder
        why we can't live,
        walk, without falling into ditches and graves?
Quickly, you default to
        degrading
        belittling
        beheading
        due to our poor decisions.
Forgetting that we are perfectly made by God
        but allowed to be imperfect.
We are not flawless.
Yet, you allow those broken pieces
        to determine my worth instead of the Creator.
Beauty is hidden
        because of your inability to see me as He sees me.

Why do you see me as . . .
        incomprehensible?
        unlovable?
        unforgivable?
My emotions impaired my vision.
Nearsighted.
No glory detected for these afflictions.
Open wounds make it hard
        for me to see through these bandages.

How quickly do you throw away what God deems worthy?
This same God Who saved you can't somehow save me.
Never forgotten.
Never a burden.

His agape love is freely given to everyone
     but somehow some of us are too damaged to receive.
That doesn't mean we are meant to be collected next week,
     then cast on a pile to decompose.
You must replicate our God,
     how He loves: without conditions or expectations.
Permission to receive grace and mercy
     when I stumble or fall on this journey.
We must not forget that unfathomable love
     embraces you despite the stench.
Declaring I smell like roses,
     calling out my potential.
We don't broadcast our mishaps.
Covering the multitude in the midst of us figuring it out.
We must always carry that Neosporin love,
     nurturing and healing balm removing any evidence of wounds.

Instead of calling me out of my name,
     help me reclaim my identity.
Always speak life into me.
Represent the God of you and me.

Never Had to Fit In

Picture This Poetry Freestyle
(Image was a photograph from childhood revealing the thickness and
length of my natural hair)

I wish she knew . . .
   that the beautiful tresses extending from her crown
   were never meant to be tamed.
Easily managed can lead to damage.
Easily managed doesn't increase your value,
   add to beauty.
The need, thought of her existence
   was lavished in beauty.
She was formed in her mother's womb in beauty.
All textures and patterns are adorned.
No need to mourn what God gave you,
   alter what has always been true.

I wish she knew . . .
   she was always worthy.
Never meant to carry the dirt and shame
   of any memories
   seeking to strip her innocence.
She was never to blame.
Insane to believe she could do anything
   to change the behaviors of others.
Wounded souls hurt each other.
A casualty of someone else's war could never
   erase the lineage of royalty.
The crown may be crooked, stained, or damaged.
Still a representation of supremacy.

I wish she knew . . .
    she never had to fit into a box,
    she would discover years later
    containment was never made for her.
I wish she knew . . .
    she could be herself and love herself
    and not crawl in the skin of others.
Blending in when again she was never meant to conform.
She was meant to create her own norm,
    a trendsetter
    a trailblazer
Inspiring multiple generations.
Never meant to fit into the world's puzzle.
God created each individual in His image,
    His likeness.
Snowflakes with a level of impact
    causing blizzards, avalanches.
Uniquely overcoming this world by storm.

You Will Never Be Enough for Them

For some people, you will never be enough.
For some people, you are too much.
You will never have the right strut or
    wear the right fit.
Your tone is always abrasive or
    doesn't reflect the right dialect or complexion.
Being assertive reeks of arrogance.
Brilliance isn't expected.
Boldness is equated to delusion.
The uneasiness in their soul deflects healing,
    fooling you into thinking you're the problem.

For some people, you will never be enough.
For some people, you are too much.
They don't understand the confidence you display.
Walking through storms determined to be the sunshine.
Overcast by the storms raging in them daily.
They cannot see you shining.
Forgetting the sun still shines even when
    you can only see the brightness of a lightning strike
    in the darkest of days.

Again, I say, don't dim your light
    for some people who think you will never be enough,
    for some people who think you are too much.
Blowing their minds with your level of audacity to believe
    you are strong enough to achieve anything,
    yet weak enough to accept assistance.
Their glass can't contain anything if it is broken.
Their perception isn't clear.
The shades on their eyes attempt to cast lies:
    you're too dim

you're too bright.
For some people, you will never be enough.
For some people, you are too much.

A treasure they wish
       they discovered within themselves.
Never demean your greatness
       based on someone else's opinion.
Their lack of validation is
       a pebble to your foundation,
       rock solid,
       unwavering in the fact your existence
       was written in heaven, predestined,
       called and equipped to handle every challenge.
Don't allow their lack of knowledge
       to taint your perception of your greatness.

Their questions can push you off the ledge.
Remember you have the ability to fly.
Keep soaring!
Keep believing!
Never should it be your mission
       to convince them of anything.
Never allow their insecurities
       to mold you into a figure contradicting
       the plan and purpose not created by man,
       a destiny curated for you
       before you were wonderfully made
       in your mother's womb.

Freely embrace wholeness,
       a reverence of your essence,
       never hiding from the ignorance
       of some people

who think you are never enough
    or think you are too much.
Never cater to an insatiable appetite
    to find what's wrong
    rather than what is right.
Allow them to have a seat,
    maybe have a taste
    to witness the feast of abundance.

We Get Lonely

They'd be lying to you
if they said they don't get lonely.
Lived long enough . . .
Experienced enough . . .
Witnessed too many others . . .
allow loneliness to smash the gas,
speed through the stop sign,
allow our longing to create a mirage,
morphing stop signs into yield signs.
Ignoring the dead-end signs.
Destined to end before it began.
Leading to disappointment,
heartache that could have been avoided.
Now in a place of contentment.
Healed and whole, we can't consume anything toxic.
Refusing to ignore everything telling us
it isn't worth it.
A piece of anything isn't worth forfeiting our peace.

Awakening
(extended Haiku)

I could smell vomit.
Erasing the stench, cleansing
My soul healing, growth.

Aware I can no
longer adapt to low
living, higher ground.

I own, rock, my crown.
Honoring beauty and flaws.
I value myself.

She Said What She Said

She said what she said.
No dread or regret in the words.
You flinch when it hits your spirit.
Your body language can't hide the blow.
You know she meant it.
She said no.
Always expected her to say yes.
Bewildered.
She will no longer tolerate anyone
    disregarding her crown.
Yet, apprehensive, expecting the same reaction.
It is hard for some to hear her say no.
Speaking to a woman who is awakened to her authority,
    no timidity resides within her.
Refusing to succumb to others' idiotic ideologies.
No longer settling for anything less than infinite.
No longer naive or hoping you don't know better.
She can sense that you did mean something,
    attempting to bring negative attention.
Microaggressions resound disrespect louder
    than a slap across the face.
She isn't standing there long enough to listen.
An audience can form but isn't needed.
She said what she said.
She knows you heard her CLEARLY.
No explanation.
No justification.
Standing on business.
She said what she said.

The Best Thing that Ever Happened to Me

He said he was the best thing that ever happened to me.
He puffed his chest out like
    what he said would cause me not to leave.
I had to let this heathen know
    he could have been the best thing
    that ever happened to me
    if I continued to have low self-esteem.
It wasn't that long ago
    I didn't know wholeness was
    never associated with desperation.
Love should have never been used
    as a potion causing dependency.

Aggravation.
Starvation.
A leech who sucked me dry.
Living a life where you dictated every move.
Lost who I was.
Caught up in catering to you.
Erasure was your definition
    of love damaging my soul.
Forgetting my purpose.
No one ever deserves this type of treatment.

Something about hitting rock bottom
    knocked me back to my senses.
Awakened me to my worth.
Clarity and sanity have returned.
No longer can I waste my time.
Invest in someone
    who doesn't reciprocate love.

The reality is you only possess the capacity
      to satisfy your insatiable appetite,
      inflate your ego.
Yes, you were the best for me.
The best to show me who not to love.
Through your inadequacy to see me
      I became awakened to my beauty.
I am a treasure who deserves better.
Adorned and admired.
Sought after.
I am beautiful.
Alone I can love myself.
Heal.
Be open to someone who understands love.
He will value who I am.
Honor what I have to offer.

I guess you are right.
You are the best thing that ever happened to me.
Because of you, I am free.

Talk that Talk

Ain't no stuntin'.
Ain't no competition.
Runnin' in my own lane
in my own race.
My pace is equivalent to the path
my Dad has laid out for me.
A journey He destined from the beginning.
Yes, I am winnin',
grinnin' from ear to ear.
Doesn't matter what catastrophe draws near.
His joy is the strength,
pushing me through every finish line.
My time to shine is now and forever.
I am the carrier of the glory from heaven.
Purposed only to draw all to Him.
Wrapped in His love.
I am His.
I am because He is.
I can because He did.
Victory is automatic
as long as I abide in Him.

Equity
(extended haiku)

Wealth gaps don't exist.
Gender isn't a box checked.
Equal playing fields.

Opportunities
open the door for others
to shine brightly too.

A chance is all we
need to prove we are really
smarter than you all.

Undaunted

Guaranteed
The sun will set and rise again.
His thoughts toward me
outnumber the grains of sand.
Assured the tide will either be high or low.
Any wind may blow.
I am undaunted, unwavering.
Standing firm in His promises.
He has favored me with abundant living.
He is faithful.

The Shift

While knowing
God created the universe,
believing the sky is the limit
was being small-minded.
Yet, standing on this balcony
has shifted my perspective.
I'm amazed at the levels of elevation.
Heights and floors that are representations of
our potential,
our greatness.
They just seem endless.
When you realize the depth of the sky,
I am reminded there is nothing
small or insignificant
about you and your purpose.

Love Thy Self

With a mocktail in hand,
I can stand
to be in my own company.
Alone but never lonely.
Completely at peace
with how dope I am.

Wholeness

There is something about being healed.
Your soul can feel your heartbeat.
No scar tissue.
No blockages to stop the flow of abundance.
Free to fulfill the rhythm of your soul.
Wholeness doesn't make you blind to negativity.
No longer underestimating your ability to withstand
      any bad vibes pushing you off the ledge
      into your demise.
You just fly.
Spread your wings in another dimension,
      on another level.
Carried.
Covered.
The One who has created you has
      strengthened you
      empowered you.
Believe everything He says about you.

It is something about being healed.
Being totally in control of your thoughts.
Negativity isn't allowed to nullify
      or override the fact
      God is in control.
The Author and Finisher
      Who holds your life in His hands
      drew out the plan to prosper.
Looks can be deceiving,
      but you continue to keep trusting.
Remembering this isn't the first or the last time
      He will show Himself strong.

Even when He tells you to let go,
        jump . . .
        it doesn't matter where you land.
Never will it be sinking sand.
Always anchored,
        grounded on that unmovable,
        impenetrable rock.
Never wavering,
        forever persevering.
Guaranteed wins,
        abundance.

It is something about being healed.
It doesn't matter what you think about me.
It doesn't matter what you say about me.
Your opinions don't validate my existence.
Your opposition doesn't disqualify me
        when I have already been
                called
                qualified
                chosen.
My crown, my eminence, isn't tainted.
You don't have to get it.
You can refuse to acknowledge it.
Affirmed and wrapped up in purpose,
        given before you formed an opinion.

I Know Better

I see you staring,
    waiting for me
    to accept the invitation:
    come over,
    start a conversation.
Hesitant
    to acknowledge your presence.
My girls tell me I need to loosen up.
It's not that serious.
Girl, you need to start living.
Have fun while dating.
They don't realize
    I don't like playing with hearts.
Unless I have spades in my hand,
    there is no need for us
    to entertain what will be
    when I know in the end
    I will renege on any promise.
Not trying to have you
    wishing you never met me like Carl Thomas.
Incapable of love at this moment.
Bruised and worn from life.
Seeking healing.
I can't rely on you.
No, this lady can't allow you to be her superman.
Turning to the one Who died on the cross for this purpose.
Allowing Him to purify my heart
Make it right for you or whoever is the man in my life.
Yes, everyone has flaws.
I know mine too well will turn into claws
    that will shred any hope of us.

Lapse in Judgment

I was content with who you were.
Never wanted to change you.
Knowing your last name would never be mine.
Deep down in the abyss of my thoughts,
     a fantasy conjuring up images of
     you and me living the life people dream.
A chocolate couple hearing we complement each other.
Holding hands, making plans
     to forever create our own Love Jones soundtrack.
You meet my family, and I meet yours.
Easily connected.
Something you said let me stay longer than needed,
     complimenting my anatomy.
Feeding my ego,
     pushing it to the forbidden zone.
Forgetting I am no longer that woman
     seeking affirmation due to insecurities.

No longer will I allow loneliness to lock me
     into strong arms that don't have the heart
     or capacity to love me.

Good conversation, escapades mean nothing
     if commitment isn't on the table
     I seek to eat from.
I must forget everything in my imagination.
You are not the one.
I can't equate my fascination,
     what some would deem hallucination
     as a guaranteed fact
     like the sun rising and setting.

Relinquishing these feelings:
     you will ever be mine.
Life is so much more than being someone's fantasy
     or holding tight to one
     that will eventually cause your heart to bleed.
I deserve to be someone's reality of love-ever-after.
Can't chase after my own version of the chapter.
The Master has a plan, and you weren't included.
A fool to alter the destination
     when the Creator is the Author of navigation.
Never meant to be a passenger on this journey.

Keep Straight

I almost veered off.
Almost took that exit.
Almost GPS'd your address.
Crazily, I remember the city.
One main street that would easily lead me back to you.
What kept me from steering in your direction was
    I said I was through.
Identified you as a blockade.
Ironically, when I stepped away and said I was done for real,
the blessings burst through like a dam,
    quenching the thirst of my soul,
    parched and tormented when connected with you.
A joyride I fooled myself into believing I was receiving—
    grieving my spirit
    draining any goodness
    erasing my common sense.
Lacking wholeness, needing to feel wanted
    morphed my psyche into believing
    what we shared was a good time.
My mind is clear,
    better off without you.
Who am I to miss or willingly be hypnotized into
    accepting lies that this situationship was ever to my advantage?
Forgetting that I am fully awake, alert to my worth.
Ain't ever accepting misuse and abuse of my affection.
The reality is I cared for you.
Disappointed that I cared more for you than myself.
Mishandled.
Never loved.
Fulfilling a feeling, something I was desperately craving.
I realize now I am complete without you.
My heart is whole without you.

When my mind sadly wants to wonder,
        wander back down memory lane
        I am careful not to beautify any disfigured memories
        only associated with rage because I overstayed in a place
        equivalent to a landfill.
I have to tell my heart to chill when
        I think about taking that exit . . .
        veering off a cliff that will end my life.
Nothing about us radiated light.

Like Fire

Passion is like fire.
Fueled by excitement.
Determine to exude greatness.
We must be intentional with
whom we share our space.
Only welcome those who edify, inspire.
Never do they extinguish your dreams.
They only seek to see you win,
blazing a trail, allowing newness to grow.

Pep Talk

She is me.
Boldly exhibiting
I am deserving of the crown
even before He knew
I would allow sin
to be my downfall.
Still He calls, qualifies.
Never believes the lies
my mistakes devalue the image
of His perfection
I was created in.
Destined to win!
Get back up!
Life is mine
to triumph with Him!
Get back up,
Sis, and win.

I Still Laugh

I laugh despite the pain.
Others would go insane.
Jesus on my membrane.
He reigns,
giving me victory over everything.
I can't buckle.
Pressure produces diamonds.
Yes, sometimes I feel like crying.
Running to the nearest exit.
No, I didn't sign up for this.
Comes with the territory.
Trusting in the Author and Finisher of my story.
Trials, tribulations won't compare to the glory
overshadowing the pain,
causing others to marvel
at His name and His wondrous ways.
Praising Him who delivers me—us—
from them all.

Staircases

Staircases
obstacles
hurdles
people
are just
stepping stones
to the
GOAL,
the DESTINY.
GREATER than any threat is the
REWARD
I already see in my mind.
DETERMINED
to lay eyes on the
PRIZE
while experiencing
VICTORY.
The journey is a process,
EMPOWERING,
EQUIPPING me.
Nothing is stopping me.

If I
BELIEVE,
FIGHT,
CONFESS,
mine it is.
Moving mountains.
CONQUERING
all trials and tribulations.
I am
BUILT

for this.
Created to REIGN.
QUEEN.
My God resurrected a
GODDESS
reflecting His authority.

These Kids Today...

These kids today ...
These kids today ...
Sometimes I feel like the older generation
      wants to label you with disgrace
      while forgetting someone gave them
      grace in the days
      wisdom seemed to evade their choices.
I need them to think, speak, then paint rainbows.
The promises of God are yes and amen.
The power in our words can dispel any cloudy days.

I need these kids . . .
      you kids . . .
      despite someone being heartless . . .
      command your destiny.
Manifest your dreams.
Break all the stereotypes by speaking life.
Hype yourself to believe
      you are the answer,
      the solution this world has been missing.
You are inventors.
You are designers.
You are architects.
You are engineers.
You are artists.
You are the leaders of today.
Your potential is drenched in greatness.

Adults, you must continue to pour water
      on the seeds continuously blooming prosperity
      no man can cut down.
Yielding a harvest no plowmen can maintain.

Sometimes I reflect on the contributions of Allen Iverson.
He was called the answer but
    at the same time the NBA wanted to bash
    something they did not contrive,
    not realizing he was birthing a shift,
    allowing people to see a face,
    a culture representative
    that was long ignored, muffled, stagnated.
Years later he was appreciated.
What we must remember is
    he didn't bend to any cheers or boos.
Headstrong, he knew all along of his greatness.

Despite the world being cruel,
    darts being hurled in the form of ridicule.
    you remember what you've been always been destined to do:
    empower
    illuminate
    orchestrate any dream
    dominate in every area
    you have been gifted to be a blessing.

You may not be liked.
You may not be respected or appreciated.
Opinions don't negate the gift inside of you.
Wonderfully made in your mother's womb.
No accident.
On purpose you were brought into this world
    to spark
    to regenerate
    to carry on a legacy for many to repeat.

These kids today . . .
You kids today . . .

You leaders today . . .
	you are exactly what we need.

Dreams

I used to get caught up in my dreams.
Make-believe to me.
Never believed they would come true.
That is why I called them dreams.
Honestly, that is the definition of a fantasy.
Something that won't become a reality,
  unattainable desires you let linger in your psyche.

Connecting with Langston Hughes
  and one of the most important messages
  from the Good News.
I realized the power of my dreams.
Deliberately envisioning goals
  aligning with His purpose.
Speaking into fruition everything
  God trusted me to manage.
Manifestation starts with dreams.
No longer using daydreaming to escape.
If I keep pushing forward,
  I can make it to my destination.

No longer wasting brain space.
Frivolous thoughts will not distract me from
  thinking, seeing, speaking, and confirming
  all God has for me.
Some call it optimism.
I call it realism.
His plans for me are yes and amen.
I am keeping my mind open
  while focused,
  meditating on His Word.
The same Word that created the universe.

The same Word that created this earth
    and all that it encompasses.

Again, I am not simply imagining
    but drawing the blueprint to be created,
    executing God's perfect plan for my life.

Breath

I hang my head to breathe.
No defeat in this stance.
Giving myself the opportunity to
        inhale and exhale the certainties,
        the dreams, and realities of winning.
Meditating on His promises.
Rehearsing my victories.
Resting because toiling isn't my norm.
My birthright involves a garden.
I lie still so He can strengthen, affirm this
        goal digger
        achiever
        motivator.
Sometimes you just have to stand and breathe.
Defeat is not in my stance.
The odds against me are my staircase
        bringing me closer to my reality.
Created for greatness.
Listening to directives
        from the One who carved out this path.
Orchestrated my narrative,
        a hopeful and prosperous future.

The Power of a Name

Dedicated to the legacy of Dr. Martin Luther King Jr that started with the name his parents gave him.

Parents, guardians,
    be intentional with how you name your children,
    be intentional with what you call them.

The power of life and death are in your tongue.

Purposely awaken the potential.
Command greatness to rise with
    so much power no man can stifle it.
Jealousy, envy, and hate can't negate
    the brilliance and magnificence.
No weapon can harm, hinder, or
    permanently dismantle their eminence.

They will inspire others.
They will empower others.
They will impact others.
Strengthen others to exhibit their dominion.
Influence a nation to carry on a dream,
    a legacy that will never die.

Am I Allowed to Just Be Me?

Literary reflection after reading Nikki Grimes's Garvey's Choice

Force feeding anyone never leads to enjoyment.
Indigestion and acid reflux are evidence something is wrong.
When will you stop trying to sell an image that is your obsession?
Your hunger has destroyed my appetite.
Chasing dreams you are desperately trying to relive.
The reality is my heart doesn't
     beat the same rhythm,
     isn't shaped the same way.

It's not that I don't admire you.
I don't want to be you or who you used to be.
I can't keep molding myself into someone I am not.
Am I allowed to be who I am,
     not who you want me to be?
Not who you hope me to be?
Not who you pretend to be
     while living through every lost memory,
     chance, and opportunity?
I just want to be me.

Whether it's football, baseball, boxing, arts, engineering,
     or everything in between
     or the fact that I am not producing the grades
     or work ethic you are used to seeing.
Am I allowed to just be me?

Am I allowed to see my own future?
Create a legacy that isn't all about boosting your ego?
Create my own destiny
     without you interfering, enforcing your ideology
     that was never meant for me?

I am not ignoring your wisdom.
I am not ignoring your advice.
Man of integrity I will always be.

Again, am I allowed to just be the person God called me to be,
    not the person you hope me to be?
Not the dreams you deferred?
Not the fantasies of reliving your glory days through me?

Am I allowed to just be me?
Exist in the purpose and plan of our Creator, our Father
    Who only gave me to you as a gift to cherish
    and steer in the right direction,
    following the roadmap from heaven.
Never intended to be a complete reflection of a parent
    who is more concerned with duplication
    versus flourishing as one's best self
    while mirroring qualities of the village.
Allowed to follow in your footsteps,
    but the footprint can be different.
Never were we meant to copy anyone else's assignment.

Fathers

Superheroes don't have to wear capes.
They help create,
shape your existence.
They save the day by
loving you,
teaching you,
cheering on their champions.
Instilling character traits like resilience.
Determined to cultivate greatness, brilliance.
Yet understanding his seed was never meant to be a duplicate,
a mini-me.
His seed was designed to be whoever
God created him or her to be.

Motherhood

A gift.
A calling.
Some would say raising.
Some would say nurturing.
We have been entrusted to
    cultivate
    devote
    dedicate
    our heart, mind, and soul
    into a being who must know
    they were carefully handcrafted in His image.
Our only purpose is to bring glory to Him.

We understand the assignment
    that is more than just raising.
More than sharing the same physical attributes.
He, she looks just like you.
It is more than having another seed
    carry the family name.
We are creating legacy
    to reverberate the blessing
    over multiple generations.
A lineage that trusts in the Author and Finisher.
We are not distracted by
    any picture or illusion
    the enemy wants to project.

We are educating,
    equipping disciplined instruments who
    will play their notes, their key, their scales
    within everlasting harmony,
    causing all demons to flee.

Forever victoriously, abundantly, dominating
        as blessings because
        we understand the assignment.
Never perfect but we don't neglect to be
        aligned with God's plan.
We are to inhabit this earth with our brilliance,
        the magnificence illuminating every room.
Exuding pride because we are fulfilling the assignment.
Moms, we are the reason why they are champions,
        mirroring the teachings
        or simply witnessing,
        studying how we didn't allow circumstances to change
        our stance that God is Jehovah Jireh, Provider.

Prayer is key.
The communication they speak.
They watch us on bended knees
        or mark our territory through
        screams and shouts,
        marching to the beat of triumph.
Mom, speaking in tongues and laying of hands,
        breaking up the land for miracles
        to continually bloom.

Yes, I salute us.
Up sleepless nights due to feedings,
        teething, doctoring, nursing.
Kissing boo-boos or hugs just because.
Fighting back tears drenched with joy,
        anguish, or frustration.
Mom, Taxi, Uber, and Lyft driver.
When they want to quit, we are their biggest cheerleader.
Meal prepping, cooking lessons in the kitchen,
        posting first day pics.

Potty training triumphs,
 loving them through break-ups.
Coaching them through that play
 before and after practice.
Turning into an actress to help them before rehearsals.
Being the loudest
 in the room,
 on the sidelines,
 in the audience
 screaming for another encore,
 with that voice they know distinctly
 THAT IS MY BABY!
The smile beaming brightly spotted from afar.
Tired, I know we sometimes are,
 but there is no place we would rather be
 than tea parties, bowling,
 or on the couch watching their favorite show.
Present and engulfed in their presence.
Sacrifice is the love language not all can articulate.
Absence is a feeling no child should have to interpret.

Unwavering in our promise
 to be their first representative of God on the earth.
Before they were birthed,
 we were, are forever grateful He chose us
 to educate, equip, discipline instruments who
 play their notes in their key and their scales
 within everlasting harmony
 while forever victoriously,
 abundantly, dominating as blessings.

My Help

I look up to the hills from which comes my help.
My God is bigger than
any problems
obstacles
or circumstances dealt.
In His hands, I am never neglected.
Forever protected!
He works it out for the best for those who love Him.
There is no limit.
On the cross, He said that it is finished.
Making it official I am victorious.

Illuminating

Illuminating
I am light overpowering darkness.
Radiating a confidence:
this crown fits me perfectly.
Deemed worthy by the King who loves me.
Died for me.
Equipping and strengthening this vessel to
conquer
create
dominate.
Reign in every arena assigned to my journey.
Beautifully handcrafted for a purpose.
My reason for dwelling on this earth.
Persevering through any pain, trial, or tribulation.
Glorious victory outweighs the hurt.
I am a fortress.
Only trusting in Him who created me,
His Masterpiece.

Never Stop

Discouraged, maybe.
Distracted temporarily.
Never dismantled from the calling that's on my life.
This crown stays intact.
Despite the scratches and bruises, my worth is still high.
Never was it tied to success.
Always interwoven into my existence.
Significance was attached to my Father's thought of me
        long before conception.
Understanding my value.

Connected to my source empowers me to see things differently.
Others may deem blocks as permanent stop signs.
My mind has been transformed to believe
        they are stumbling blocks only meant to build a staircase
        bringing me closer to the promise.
As I abide in Him, everything He said I can have is mine.
I will continue to shine
        despite feeling like I am surrounded by darkness.
Even with my eyes closed, I see light.

Faith confirms with my spirit the way
        He carved out for me
        is paved with prosperity and longevity.
I am not just talking about money growing on trees.
Wealth that produces ideas breaking through any market.
The favor causing people to give freely
        when they don't understand or don't believe I am deserving.
Blessed and graced to face every situation and circumstance.
Enabled to execute what some would deem as risks or impossible.
Experience with my Savior has added more wins
        in the column than losses.

I can't get caught up in what seems to be defeat.
Everything always works out for me.
As a result, I can't stop shining.

Deeper Than I Love You

This is deeper than saying I love you.

Hearts beat in sync.
The pattern can't be mimicked.
A union God created,
    destined before the beginning of time.
His purpose, his plan for man to love his wife
    like Christ loves the church.
There is no undervaluing how much
    you,
    I,
    us
    is worth.

We are intertwined.
Amazing how you know what is on my mind.
I know what is on yours.
We can laugh without words exchanged.
I can hear and feel your stride
    without setting eyes on the joy of my life.
You smile when you hear me strut
    in heels, sneakers, or boots.
The softness of your lips keeps
    honey on our moon
    even when we have to make room
    for baby weight,
    metabolism slowing down
    as we enter our 30s.
Comfortable to be ourselves
    while embracing, accepting
    I may sometimes wear a bonnet to sleep.
    You may forget to lower the toilet seat.
    I leave on the lights

despite not being in the room.
I can never make up my mind
when it is time to get food.

I get you.
You get me.
My love language
	you interpret effortlessly.
Your love language
	I understand perfectly.
Do for you like you do for me.
We aren't patting backs or keeping score.
My world
Your world
	would lack if
	I,
	you
	didn't make
	you,
	me
	happy.

Valentine's Days and birthdays
	are the icing on the cake.
Every day we experience
	what some dream and fantasize about.
What the movies, love songs, and poems
	try to romanticize.
Adoration.
You are mine.
I am yours.
Forever.
Always.
Until infinity and beyond.

The massiveness of the universe
        can't equate to our more-than-forever love.

Unbreakable.
No fight or disagreement can rip or devalue
        what God called a good thing.
Refuse to go to bed angry,
        confusing the enemy.
Not saying you won't aggravate me.
Sometimes we clearly need space.
Only to end up in each other's embrace.
Again, we may not be able
        to hash it out immediately.
Processing while not letting
        anger rule our tongues.
Apologizing while empathizing.
Can't give the devil any room.
This is deeper than saying I love you.

Prayer is critical to operate
        in abundance.
Our steps are ordered down a path
        covered in favor,
        securing each other and our seeds.
We're doing this thing called life together.
Conquering this world together.
Braving the storms:
        bad doctor's reports
        our children resorting to behaviors
        we didn't teach them.

Encircled in your love,
        the warmth of your arms reminds
        me, us there is no need to be alarmed.

Your head nestled in my bosom
        brings a peace surpassing all understanding.
We can't second-guess this union.
We trust in the one Who strengthens us.
All things work together because He loves us.
Unmovable like the tree planted by the river.
Proving to the world marriage is real and works.

This covenant is sealed.
A promise to indulge, create joy.
A partnership sprouting roots and seeds,
        creating a legacy.
Our heritage, our lineage
        will impact,
        inspire the world,
        to be carried on through multiple generations.
Two families connecting.
Extending heaven's blessing.
More laughs at the
        dinner table,
        family reunions,
        Thanksgivings,
        and Christmases.
Creating our own traditions.
Matching jerseys while watching sports on TV.
Forever my spades partner.
Always my plus one.
My dance partner
        even when there is only us humming
        a tune in the middle of a room.
No permission needed to be in the moment.
Always and forever,
Object of my affection.

The subject of my love letter,
    longer than four pages.
In stages, we will grow.
Time will continue to show.
This is deeper than saying I love you.

Storms End with Rainbows

When we become one,
love covers, shields, heals, protects.
Dignity revealed.

Humanity still exists.
Never neglecting our duty,
a desire to be a blessing.
Answering the call.
Fulfilling every need.

Never meant to be isolated but
united, strengthened.

Dare to believe you don't have to have all the answers.
People can bring clarity or a sense of peace surpassing understanding.
A shoulder, a listening ear of the frustrations that seek to break you.
We won't let it take your joy.

Restoration is upon those who believe and accept victory.

No, this isn't the end but a new beginning.
A glorious sunrise shining bright over the disasters of life.
Triumph runs through your veins, so I say again ...

You are still winning.
You are still living bravely.
Storms end with rainbows.

No Needy Among Us

In Acts 4:34, there were no needy among them.
The community eliminated any need.
Our hearts need to resound that same benevolence.
Blessing our fellow man so there are no needy amongst us.
Whether it is eliminating food deserts
        instituting more programs
        eliminating crime and violence.
Silence can no more be accepted
        when our community has needs unmet.
No longer can we mind our business
        when it has always been our business,
        purpose to look after each other.
Reemerging the village.
Blessed to be a blessing.

Beautiful lesson we can also exhibit from Acts 4 :34:
        no one was afraid, ashamed, or too prideful
        to admit to shortcomings.
No one was willing to accept that is just the way it is.
They felt comfortable airing their grievances.
Assured and wrapped in the support of their community,
        who realized we are all one entity.
We are afflicted when there is scarcity among us.
Again, we must get back to a place
        where the strength of an embrace
        erases the shame and fear of someone's name
        being dragged through the mud
        because they cried out for help.
An outcry petitioning we should have a sense of urgency
        while doing whatever is necessary:
        goods, services, and resources.
Let's reestablish the trust between us.

We got us.
We can no longer afford to drown out
        the pleas of our community:
        all voices, races, ethnicities, genders, and religions.
Me coming from a Christian household shouldn't
        place a chokehold on those seeking to just breathe.
Despite our differences,
        we must listen
        then take action
        so there is no need among us.
Equity and equality are no longer dreams deferred.

We will no longer feel like we are speaking, singing the lies we learned.
No longer can we lip sync or mimic harmony disguised as discord.
We must, we can, and we shall believe this land is truly our land.
Representing the true essence, the fabric of our being.
Lifting up every voice
        while remembering we shouted WE
        not just me and my family but we, the nation,
        declaring a new song reverberating a rhythm,
        cadence representing all people.
Resembling again Acts chapter 4:34.

There were no needy among them.
There are no needy among us.
Our ultimate purpose is to be servants.

Bibliophile
(extended haiku)

Imagination
sparked by placement of words, lines.
A brilliant journey.

I can't grow without
knowing how my ancestors
conquered, flourished, reigned.

Place where Blackness can
overpower white pages.
No opposition.

Chosen
(extended haiku)

Kings and queens who rise
despite hate and ignorance.
Never deny light.

Disqualified, no.
Mistakes don't nullify or
erase eminence.

Resilience is the
heartbeat invigorating
our spirit to win.

Choosing Joy

I smile . . .
knowing this world isn't perfect.
Filled with people who inflict
pain no one deserves.
Yet, I smile, resembling
an upside-down rainbow.
Cognizant of God's promises.
Some would call it favor, a covering.
Yes, promises I am confident
He will continue to fulfill.

I WILL NOT BE SILENT

Poetic version of Phil Thompson's "My Worship"

And I will not be silent
I will always worship You
As long as I am breathing
I will always worship You
And I will not be silent . . .
No, I can't keep quiet.
I can't allow the rocks to cry out.
I can't allow you not to hear about
    how awesome and wonderful my God is.
When I think about my blessings, my child, my family,
    my mother,
    my father who's gone on before me,
    my brother, my sister,
    my son, my students, my job,
    I can't be silent.
Countless times He has delivered, set me free
    from the traps of the enemy or my stupidity.
2019 I was unexpectedly hospitalized with something
    that sought to be my demise.
At one point I couldn't write, my psyche wasn't right.
Now here I stand, the author and publisher of seven books.
Reading, performing words that bring light.
My testimony must draw all those to taste and see.
You're looking at a girl, a woman who is now whole.
Someone who used to let her life go out of control.
Once I decided to trust in the Father
    who is the Author and Finisher of my faith,
    I realized that the way is paved with gold, favor.
Grace and mercy follow me.
There's no reason for me to draw back, backslide.
Yes, your girl used to be *SILENT*,

creep and do things that would grieve the Spirit.
Intertwined with darkness, which mirrors being heartless.
Refusing to reveal I have been redeemed.
Living a life resembling ungratefulness.
Now I am fully awakened to the power within me,
          realizing I was never created to be *SILENT.*

I will always worship you.
Worship isn't me just raising my hands in the sanctuary.
Worship is how I smile at you, ask how you are doing.
Worship can be me complimenting your outfit.
Worship is the way I treat people how I want to be treated.
Worship is how I act on my job.
I do what I do as unto the Lord.
Worship is people truly experiencing my heart, God's heart.
Worship is loving my son with my whole being.
He has everything that he wants.
Worship is looking out for the needy.
Making sure no one goes hungry.
Worship is how I treat my temple.
Treasuring every blessing.
Worship is you never questioning if my love for God is genuine.
Actions reveal my relationship with Him is authentic.
Forever a representation of the Creator.
Yes, this realness screams to the heavens:
I can't be silent.
I will always worship you.

As long as I am breathing . . .
Yes, it is in Him I live, move, and have my being.
My purpose, the reason I exist is
          to bring all glory and honor to my Father
          Who had me in mind since the beginning of time.
Man and woman must exude power and light.

Never should we disconnect or unplug.
Never should we dim our greatness.
I will not let my breath go to waste.
Never again will I allow darkness to invade.
I will not let him stifle me.
I will continue to let this breath run through my lungs.
Inhaling and exhaling goodness, abundance.
Boldly declaring and thankful He's always there,
> omnipresent and omnipotent, all powerful,
> Healer, Comforter, Waymaker, Miracle Worker
> Who I will forever *worship*.

Preview of
AVOIDING THE LABEL

A collection of essays, short stories, journal entries, and poetry from a single woman seeking wholeness.

"Beautiful Yet Unsustainable"

I remember when I thought I needed you. I thought I missed something because you have always been there without a demand or request. I interpreted your never-ending presence as a silent request to open my heart to yours or a message from heaven stating that I needed you. Yet, in the craziest and most terrifying moment of my life, you were nonexistent. Vanished without a trace. I would consciously and unconsciously look for your face because I knew we were living within miles of each other. If I wanted to, I could show up at your doorstep and ask why you abandoned me. In reality, you never had the fortitude to withstand the horrific storm. No one foresaw I would have to battle back to a norm that would separate and reveal genuine connections.

I remember wanting someone out of my life so bad I made it a point not to speak his name. Somehow speaking his name would cause my phone to ring. I could never forget his area code, but I so badly needed to forget his name and the chokehold he had on my heart. Determined to forget him, I did forget his name while not answering his phone calls. He turned into that dude who I wasted months of my life with, living a lie that we needed each other.

Nevertheless, you were different. Ironically, the same action of me thinking of you, speaking of you, remembering you caused me to see you for the first time in FIVE years. Both of us were shocked to see each other, two people who enjoyed one another in the most intimate way.

Some would deem our relationship as a situationship, but we knew it meant more. Hesitant to explore due to transgressions that seemed to handicap your senses, I wanted more for you than nights dulling pain or just fading away into a river of bliss overtaking any regrets. When I finally accepted we would be nothing more than friends despite writing poems about our interactions, you remained there. When called, you came to help in any way possible while I still found it improbable for a man to be willing to help without demanding or expecting a favor in return. I had friends who were brothers, but they were also obligated to their wives. No attraction was going to pervert their obligation to help their sister. You were different: single and once my lover. We spent time under the covers and in each other's embrace. Yet, you occupied a space I didn't know existed: life after benefits. We dispelled the myth that males and females can't coexist without being overpowered by their desires. I don't remember exactly when we decided to just be, decided to extinguish the flame while holding onto memories and forming a new existence of just being friends.

That new existence left a lingering feeling that maybe I didn't try hard enough to understand exactly what you were trying to send down the river of bliss. Something hurt you. Something or someone enabled you to sometimes disappear for weeks at a time but resurface from time to time to breathe and help me. Again, I knew you didn't have to keep dealing with me, but you did. Because you did, I knew I needed to try and see what those unresolved feelings could amount to.

Never did I get that chance and yet, tonight, we stand face to face after me thinking of you, speaking of you, remembering you. Years of hoping for another chance has bubbled over and caused you to reappear in front of me. I remember imagining, wondering what it would be like if I ever saw you again. Would I pretend not to be mesmerized by the chocolate of your smooth skin and the muscles sculpting every inch of your clothes? Would we embrace? Would we end up back at either your place or mine? And in that moment, I was frozen yet grateful I finally got my wish granted to at least lay eyes on you. What was more beautiful is you didn't deem it harmful to say hello, for us to engage in a conversation I had been rehearsing for over five years.

Five years ago, I would have deemed our encounter as a chance for us to discover or finish what I attempted to uncover. I thought I had unresolved feelings. Five years ago, I was a different person who was impatient and willing to force puzzle pieces to magically fit. I am not going to say we never fit. Something about us fit for the moment, and I can't deny the beauty and passion that was ingrained in my psyche. Five years ago, I would have thrown all caution to the wind, ignoring my progress, to only give into desires that never quite left me content. Inadequate, you praised my gift to exhilarate your soul, yet I was always left conflicted and uneasy due to the lack of wholeness.

Sometimes I wonder if my brokenness blinded me to you loving me or caring for me so deeply you hung around just to see if I would come around. You said helping people was just in your nature, but there is a part of me wondering if it was done to see, waiting until I would finally see you were all I needed. Then the memories of you fleeing, escaping my storm you were never meant to save me from. Yet, you never stayed to see if I survived. I felt stranded but would later realize you were never the man I needed you to be. Reminding me I can't conjure up this lie that tonight was our chance to rediscover or rekindle any relationship.

Tonight's encounter was simply a coincidence that could easily be a distraction from the progress I have made in the past three years. What we had was beautiful yet unsustainable. I won't forget that next time.

ABOUT THE AUTHOR

For over 30 years, Rian N. Jenkins has inspired, entertained, and educated many through poetry, novellas, journalism, and performances. In 2021, she added author to her resume. As of 2025, she has self published three poetry books, two children's books—*A Blessing for The World* and *Heaven's Jewel*—and a middle grade novel, *Reverse*.

She is the mother of a brilliant young king in college, and she is a teacher, spoken word artist, podcaster, mentor, and program director of CROWN HER. She also calls herself a LIT specialist who does book talks online while sponsoring All Black Author Book Drive and Giveaway in the Columbia area.

She is a native of Sumter, SC but graduated from Ridge View in '98 and Winthrop University in '03. She also has roots in Edisto Island, Hollywood, and St Helena Island.

Learn more about her and where to find her on social media on her website, WWW.RIANNJENKINS.COM